Made in the USA
Columbia, SC
09 July 2021

41593168R00057